Fifteen Etudes for Cello, Op. 76

(with 2nd Violoncello accompaniment)

by

David Popper

Prepared for Publication by Paul Fleury

David Popper
Fifteen Etudes, Op. 76
(with 2nd Violoncello accompaniment)

Lustig bewegt (à la marcia)

Andante sostenuto

4

Lebhaft (Allegro vivace)

5

Andante grazioso

6

13

rall. poco a poco

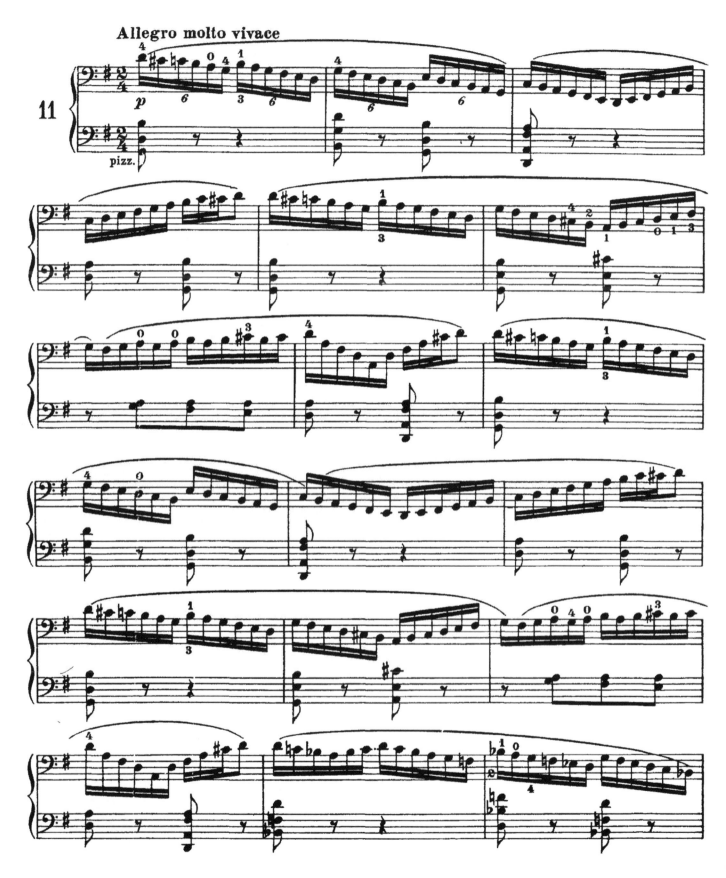

23

Gigue
Allegro molto vivo

15

NOTES

NOTES

NOTES

NOTES

Made in the USA
Middletown, DE
18 July 2020

13042310R00020